D1011153

LIFE'S LITTLE TREASURE BOOK

On Marriage AND FAMILY

H. JACKSON BROWN, JR.

RUTLEDGE HILL PRESS

NASHVILLE, TENNESSEE

Published in Nashville, Tennessee, by
Rutledge Hill Press, Inc., 211 Seventh Avenue
North, Nashville, Tennessee 37219.
Distributed in Canada by H. B. Fenn and
Company Ltd., Mississauga, Ontario.

Typography by D&T/Bailey Typesetting, Inc.,
Nashville, Tennessee
Illustrations by Cristine Mortensen
Book design by Harriette Bateman

ISBN: 1-55853-277-3

Printed in Hong Kong through Palace Press
2 3 4 5 6 7 8 9 — 97 96 95 94

INTRODUCTION

$\mathscr{A}$ few years ago, I offered my eighteen-year-old son, Adam, this advice: "Choose your life's mate carefully. From this one decision will come 90 percent of all your happiness or misery." But after having chosen carefully, I added, the work has just begun.

A successful marriage, like a well-tended garden, takes constant care and loving attention. But the couple who spends the time to cultivate a joyful marriage and harmonious home discovers it is the best investment they can make.

Some of the entries in this little book include observations and suggestions I shared with Adam in both volumes of *Life's Little Instruction Book*. As a recent college graduate, he is giving serious thought to what it takes to be a good husband and father. He tells me these suggestions have been helpful. I hope you will find something of value here, too.

Men and women sometimes discover that finding a desirable marriage partner is difficult. That may be true. But there is another component to the situation: for it is not enough to find the right person, we must *be* the right person.

*C*hoose your life's mate carefully. From this one decision will come 90 percent of all your happiness or misery.

*M*arry only for love.

❧

*A*ll good marriages have
this in common: courtesy,
sacrifice, and forgiveness.

❧

*D*iscover a special place to
watch sunsets together.

A successful marriage requires falling in love many times, always with the same person.

— Mignon McLaughlin

A happy home
is a glimpse
of heaven.

$\mathcal{K}$iss in the rain.

❧

$\mathcal{S}$low dance.

❧

$\mathcal{I}$f you've had
a hard day at the office,
save the complaining
until after dinner.

*N*ever underestimate the
power of forgiveness.

❧

*P*ut love notes under your
spouse's pillow.

❧

Grow old along with me.
The best is yet to be.

— Robert Browning

When you and your spouse
have a disagreement,
regardless of who's wrong,
apologize. Say,
"I'm sorry I upset you.
Would you forgive me?"
These are healing,
magical words.

Spend some time alone.

❧

An archeologist is the best husband any woman could have. The older she gets, the more interested he is in her.

— Agatha Christie

$\mathcal{B}$e
the first
to forgive.

Send your loved ones
flowers. Think of
a reason later.

∾

Let your children
overhear you saying
complimentary things
about them to
other adults.

*J*udge your success
by the happiness of
your wife
and the respect
given to you
by your children.

*I*ntroduce yourself to
your neighbors as soon as
you move into a
new neighborhood.

❧

*R*emember that a good
marriage is like a campfire.
Both grow cold if
left unattended.

*H*old hands at the movies.

❧

*G*et involved at your
child's school.

❧

*N*ever leave a youngster
in the car without taking
the car keys.

Buy your fiancée the nicest
diamond engagement ring
you can afford.

❧

*Don't marry anyone
who won't bait their
own hook.*

— Wiley Dobbs

...To have and to hold
from this day forward,
for better, for worse, for
richer, for poorer,
in sickness and in health,
to love and to cherish,
till death us do part.

— The Book of Common Prayer

*R*espect your children's
privacy. Knock before
entering their rooms.

∾

*A*lways buy
electric blankets with
dual controls.

∾

*N*ever mention past loves.

Remember the observation of
William James that
the deepest principle in
human nature is the
craving to be appreciated.

Never argue in the bedroom.
This should be a sanctuary of
love, peace, and security.

Marriage resembles a pair of shears — so joined that they cannot be separated, often moving in opposite directions, yet always punishing anyone who comes between them.

— Sydney Smith

*P*lant a garden together.

❧

*N*ever be the first to break a
family tradition.

❧

How do I love thee?
Let me count the ways.

— Elizabeth Barrett Browning

As soon as you get married,
start saving for your
children's education.

~

Phone when you are
going to be late.

~

Live beneath your means.

Conduct family fire drills.
Be sure everyone knows
what to do in case
the house catches fire.

෨

Give children toys that
are powered by
their imagination,
not by batteries.

*D*on't take
good friends,
good health, or a
good marriage
for granted.

*A*dd to your children's
private library by giving them
a hardback copy of one of
the classics every birthday.
Begin with their first birthday.

❧

*D*on't discuss
domestic problems
at work.

Discipline with a gentle hand.

❧

Love does not consist in
gazing at each other,
but in looking outward
together in the
same direction.

— Antoine de Saint-Exupéry

$\mathcal{T}$hree things to look for
in a spouse:
1. a sweet disposition,
2. a sense of humor,
3. loves trips to
Home Depot.

$\mathcal{L}$et there be spaces in

your togetherness.

— Kahlil Gibran

$\mathcal{N}$ever yell at each other
unless the house is on fire.

❧

$\mathcal{R}$ead the Sunday comics
together.

*L*ive so that when your
children think of fairness,
caring, and integrity,
they think of you.

∾

*A*t least once a day tell
your wife how terrific she is
and that you love her.

*I*n disagreements, fight fairly.
No name calling.

❧

*P*ut love notes in your
child's lunch box.

❧

*L*earn to say "I love you"
in sign language.

By all means marry.
If you get a good wife,
you'll become happy;
if you get a bad one,
you'll become a
philosopher.

— Socrates

*R*emember that
your child's character is
like good soup.
Both are homemade.

❧

*W*hen you know that
someone has gone to a lot of
trouble to get dressed up,
tell them they look terrific!

$\mathcal{P}$raise in public.

❧

$\mathcal{C}$riticize in private.

❧

$\mathcal{R}$emember the two essentials
for a happy marriage:
separate bathrooms and
separate checking accounts.

*A marriage makes of two
fractional lines a whole;
it gives to two purposeless lives
a work, and doubles the
strength of each to perform it;
it gives to two questioning
natures a reason for living,
and something to live for.*

— Mark Twain

When you are away
from home and hear
church bells, think of
someone who
loves you.

❧

Tell your kids often
how terrific they are and
that you trust them.

*Remember that
no time spent with
your children is
ever wasted.*

&

*Love comforteth like
sunshine after rain.*

— William Shakespeare

*D*on't worry that
you can't give your
kids the best of everything.
Give them your very best.

∾

*I*n disagreements with
loved ones, deal with
the current situations.
Don't bring up the past.

Create a little signal
only your wife knows
so that you can show her
you love her across a
crowded room.

❧

When playing games
with children,
let them win.

$\mathcal{N}$ever waste
an opportunity to
tell someone you
love them.

*R*ead to your children.

❧

*S*ing to your children.

❧

*L*isten to your children.

*R*emember that a
good marriage is based
on commitment,
not convenience.

❧

*D*on't spend lots of time
with couples who
constantly criticize
each other.

*M*arry a woman you
love to talk to.
As you get older,
her conversational skills
will be as important
as any other.

∾

A good marriage divides
grief and multiplies joy.

$\mathcal{B}$e alert for opportunities to
show praise and appreciation.

❧

$\mathcal{T}$he husband who wants
a happy marriage should
learn to keep his mouth shut
and his checkbook open.

— Groucho Marx

Never say anything
uncomplimentary about
your spouse or children
in the presence of others.

∾

Everyone loves praise.
Look hard for ways to
give it to them.

Cherish your children for
what they are,
not for what you'd
like them to be.

❧

Send your mother-in-law
flowers on your
wife's birthday.

*R*emember that the
best relationship is
one where your
love for each other is
greater than your
need for each other.

∾

*D*on't pick up after your
children. That's their job.

*C*arry a list of
your spouse's important sizes
in your wallet.

❧

*N*ever forget the nine most
important words of
any marriage:
1. I love you.
2. You are beautiful.
3. Please forgive me.

*H*elp your children
set up their own savings
and checking accounts
by age sixteen.

❧

*B*uy your spouse a year's
subscription to his or her
favorite magazine.

Turn off the television
at dinner time.

❧

Flirt, but only with
each other.

A loving atmosphere in
your home is so important.
Do all you can to create a
tranquil, harmonious home.

∾

*W*hen you tell a child to
do something, don't follow it
with, "Okay?" Ask instead,
"Do you understand?"

*A*pproach
love and cooking
with
reckless abandon.

$\mathcal{P}$ut the cap back on
the toothpaste.

❧

$\mathcal{T}$ake out the garbage
without being told.

❧

$\mathcal{D}$on't expect others to
listen to your advice and
ignore your example.

Don't let your family
get so busy that you
don't sit down to
at least one meal
a day together.

❧

*Spoil your husband, but
don't spoil your children.*

— Louise Currey

*K*eep the porch
light on until
all the family
is in for the night.

*E*ven if you're financially
well-to-do, have your
children earn and pay part
of their college tuition.

&

*E*ven if you're financially
well-to-do, have your
children earn and pay for *all*
their automobile insurance.

*H*old your child's hand
every chance you get.
The time will come
all too soon when
he or she won't let you.

∽

*D*on't expect your love alone
to make a neat person out of
a messy one.

Champion
your wife.
Be her best friend
and biggest fan.

Set aside your dreams
for your children and
help them attain
their own dreams.

❧

Save an evening a week for
just you and your spouse.

❧

Believe in love at first sight.

The love we have in our youth is superficial compared to the love that an old man has for his wife.

— Will Durant

$\mathcal{N}$ever walk out on a quarrel.

∾

$\mathcal{D}$on't judge people by
their relatives.

∾

$\mathcal{N}$ever discuss important
matters with the
television on.

Love deeply and passionately.
You might get hurt,
but it's the only way to
live life completely.

❧

A successful marriage
is an edifice that must be
rebuilt every day.

— Andre Maurou

Never miss a chance to
dance with your spouse.

❧

Surprise your wife by
vacuuming and
washing her car.

❧

Never say, "My child would
never do that."

When a woman decides
she wants something,
don't underestimate her
ability to get it.

❧

Know when to keep silent.

❧

Know when to speak up.

*M*arriage is
an empty box.
It remains empty
unless you put in
more than
you take out.

*I married my husband
for better or worse,
but not for lunch.*

— Leigh Carleton

*G*o on blind dates.
Remember, that's how I
met your mother.

❧

*T*ake good care of
those you love.

❧

*S*urprise loved ones with
little unexpected gifts.

*B*e your children's best
teacher and coach.

❧

*E*very day look for
some small way to
improve your marriage.

❧

*B*e romantic.

When a child falls and
skins a knee or elbow,
always show concern;
then take the time to
"kiss it and make it better."

❧

Never give a loved one a
gift that suggests he or she
needs improvement.

*A*llow your children to
face the consequences of
their actions.

❧

*T*ake family vacations
whether you can afford
them or not.
The memories will
be priceless.

When your children are
learning to play
musical instruments,
buy them good ones.

∾

Let your spouse overhear you
saying complimentary things
about him or her to
other people.

A hundred men may
make an encampment,
but it takes a woman to
make a home.

— Chinese Proverb

*A*ttend your children's
athletic contests,
plays, and recitals.

∾

*B*efore going to bed on
Christmas Eve,
join hands with
your family and sing
"Silent Night."

*H*ug your children after
you discipline them.

∾

*M*emorize your spouse's
favorite love poem.

$\mathcal{R}$emember that a woman
never gets tired of hearing
these words: "I love you,"
"I cherish you," "I'm so lucky
to have found you."

∾

$\mathcal{T}$each your children the
value of money and the
importance of saving.

$\mathcal{N}$ever type a love letter.
Use a fountain pen.

❧

$\mathcal{D}$on't scrimp in order to
leave money to your children.

❧

$\mathcal{R}$eally celebrate your
anniversary. Make it an
all-day event.

$\mathcal{B}$uy a new tie to wear to
your wedding rehearsal dinner.
Wear it only once.
Keep it forever.

❧

$\mathcal{R}$emember that
great love and
great achievements
involve great risk.

$\mathcal{L}$earn to say
"I love you" in
French, Italian, and Swedish.

∾

$\mathcal{N}$ever buy a house without
a fireplace.

∾

$\mathcal{D}$on't let family members
drive on slick tires.

Exercise together.

❧

Dream together.

❧

Pray together.

If you can find a truly good wife, she is worth more than precious gems! When she speaks, her words are wise, and kindness is the rule for everything she says.

— Proverbs 31:10, 26 (Living Bible)

Tape record your parents' memories of how they met and their first years of marriage.

❧

A good husband should be deaf, and a good wife should be blind.

— French Proverb

*D*rive as you wish
your kids would.
Never speed or
drive recklessly with
children in the car.

❧

*M*ake the rules for
your children clear,
fair, and consistent.

*R*emember that a
successful marriage
depends on two things:
1. finding the right person
2. being the right person.

∾

*E*very year celebrate the
day you and your wife had
your first date.

Encourage your children to
have a part-time job after
the age of sixteen.

❧

Never stop the wooing.

When tempted to criticize your parents, spouse, or children, bite your tongue.

❧

I chose my wife, as she did her wedding gown, for qualities that would wear well.

— Oliver Goldsmith

Let your children see you
do things for your wife
that lets them know
how much you love
and treasure her.

❧

Open the car door for
your wife and always help her
with her coat.

$\mathcal{D}$on't overfeed horses or
brothers-in-law.

∾

$\mathcal{W}$hen angry, never begin
a sentence with,
"You always..."

∾

$\mathcal{G}$reet each other at the door
with a kiss and a hug.

I would like to have engraved inside every wedding band, 'Be kind to one another.' This is the golden rule of marriage and the secret of making love last through the years.

— Rudolph Ray

$\mathscr{B}$e your
mate's best
friend.